CW00840458

Only One World

An Autobiography by David Shepherd

Contents

Introducing myself......................................2

My childhood...4

My first trip to Africa............................ 6

    Nairobi...8

    Malindi.. 9

The big decision....................................12

My training as an artist..........................14

My early career......................................16

The turning point..................................18

Becoming a conservationist....................22

Only one world......................................30

Index..32

06732

Introducing myself

My name is David Shepherd and I am an artist. I paint pictures of steam trains, aeroplanes, English scenes and portraits but I am best known for painting pictures of African wildlife and, in particular, elephants.

It is funny to think that when I was growing up as a small boy, I had one ambition—to be a game warden in Kenya. It's funny because I had never been abroad, except for a day trip to France and back, and I knew nothing about animals whatsoever!

As a small boy, I collected books on Africa because they were very exciting to read. They were tales of adventure and exploration. Many of these books were written by the big game hunters many years ago. In those days, they had the idea that if an animal moved, it should be shot. I can remember many awful tales of this sort of behaviour.

Many of these books were long tales of slaughter, but I didn't see it that way when I read them all those years ago. I just thought it would be romantic to be a game warden. I would walk around in the fresh air all day, looking after the animals.

My childhood

I was born in 1931, in Hendon, in North London. Just after World War II started, my family moved to a house in Totteridge, a few miles away from Hendon. I lived in this house right through the war, with my brother and sister and mother. My father was away in the army. None of us children realized that people were killing each other, as we watched the fighting overhead between the British and German aeroplanes. We had some of our windows blown out by the bombing. My brother and I used to collect bits of crashed German aeroplanes. World War II was exciting and a lot of fun for a child of my age.

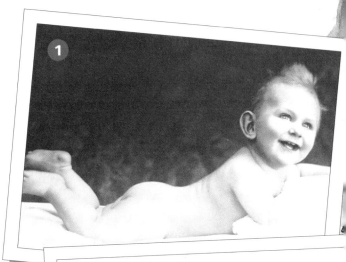

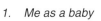

1. Me as a baby
2. Our house in Totteridge
3. Me with my brother and sister
4. Me and Mum with the dogs
5. My parents
6. Me when I was 12

I still had this one dream—to be a game warden in East Africa! I certainly never thought of being an artist. For one thing, I wasn't really interested in painting. Furthermore, I certainly had no talent. However, I did do a few paintings of birds—although I don't think they looked very much like anything that has wings!

My first trip to Africa

I left school in 1949 at the age of 18 and prepared for my great adventure in life—to go to Kenya. My father was very kind and he made no attempt to stop me. I feel so ashamed now when I think of all the trouble and money that I cost him. My belongings were all packed up in a huge crate which was sent out in advance by air— I even took my bicycle! It never occurred to either my father or myself that they have bicycles in Africa, millions and millions of them!

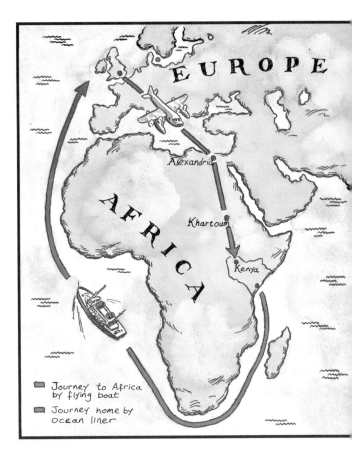

To begin with, I worked on a coffee farm in Kenya, a long way from any wildlife. I was homesick from the moment I arrived! I was miles and miles away from home and I knew no one. Furthermore, I knew nothing about coffee! The owner of the farm made it quite plain that he regarded me as useless—which I think I was. All I wanted was to come home but my father quite rightly said that I would have to stay. I had cost him all that money and he said, "You really must make an effort to grow up." After all, I was 18 years old.

I spent one miserable month on the coffee farm, by which time the owner was only too delighted to get rid of me. He had friends in Nairobi and he wrote to them and warned them that I was coming, so that they knew what to expect.

NAIROBI

At least I was now in the capital of Kenya and this was my chance to become a game warden—or at least that is what I thought! I went along to the office to meet the head game warden.

"I am here," I said.

I really did believe that they would say, "Thank goodness, we have been waiting for you". Of course, they didn't. They had no jobs to offer and they very politely told me that even if they did, I was hopelessly unqualified. After all, to say you have been to France for the day is not really enough to become a game warden anywhere. Furthermore, I hardly knew one end of an elephant from the other!

My world seemed to fall apart in ruins.

However, one of the game wardens took pity on me and he invited me to go with him to a lovely place called Amboseli. Amboseli is under the shadow of the highest mountain in Africa, Mount Kilimanjaro. There, for the very first time, I watched a herd of elephants in the wild. I felt very small, but that first great sight of elephants had a great impact on my life.

MALINDI

There I was in Nairobi, without a job, and my father would not let me come home. I answered an advertisement in a Nairobi newspaper saying that a hotel in Malindi, on the coast of Kenya, wanted someone to work for them. I knew nothing about hotels but the hotel owner seemed to like me. He offered me £1.00 a week to 'generally make myself useful'.

Hotel
Receptionist
required at
The
Sindbad
Hotel
TELEPHONE MALINDI 7

The moment I arrived at the hotel, before I had even unpacked my bags, I was asked to take a party of American tourists out snorkelling on the reef. I hardly knew what snorkelling meant. It turned out to be an exciting experience. We swam in the warm waters inside the reef away from the sharks. There we floated on the surface, looking down into the crowds of unbelievably beautiful fish. The Americans were impressed. They thought I had lived in Kenya all my life and I had only been in the hotel for 20 minutes!

Over the next six months, I generally made myself useful and also had time to paint a few terrible pictures of birds. What a joke it seems now! There I was, beside the Indian Ocean and palm trees, and I chose to paint pictures of mallards flying in over the Norfolk and Suffolk coast! However, I sold all the paintings to the local people for £10.00 each and so I was able to earn enough money to pay for my passage home on an ocean liner.

UNION-CASTLE LINE
HANDBOOK OF INFORMATION FOR PASSENGERS

MAIL & INTERMEDIATE SERVICES
BETWEEN ENGLAND AND
SOUTH AFRICA
WEST & EAST AFRICA

The big decision

I arrived home from Africa thinking that my life was a disaster. I had failed miserably to be the only thing I wanted to be, a game warden. It seemed that I now had two choices left. One was to earn a reasonable living driving a bus. The other choice was to try and be an artist—but I had no talent, wasn't really interested, and I thought I would probably starve.

My parents probably thought I would starve too, but they didn't stand in my way when I decided that I would rather be an artist than drive a bus. So off I went to an Art School in London to have some training. I showed them one of my terrible bird paintings and they promptly threw me out! They said I was not worth teaching and that I had better go off and drive a bus. So, after failing to be a game warden, it seemed that I had now failed to be an artist as well!

My bird painting!

Shortly after this, a miracle happened. I went to a party in London where I was introduced to a man called Robin Goodwin. He was a professional artist, who earned his living painting pictures for people. I started to tell him about my tale of disasters, one after another, and he offered to see my work.

I drove up to his London studio the next day with my bird painting. I fully expected him to tell me to go home and drive a bus, but he didn't. He took one look at my awful work and said, "Do you want me to teach you?" That was in 1951. I still don't know why Robin decided to teach me. He probably thought it would be a challenge to teach someone so dreadful.

My training as an artist

I spent three years with Robin Goodwin as his only student. He taught me everything I know about painting. He also taught me how to be a businessman. He pointed out that art is really no different from any other job. It is a living to earn money. Some artists think that they can only paint when they are inspired and 'feel like it'.

"Nonsense to that," Robin said. "You are going to be painting on Sundays as well as every other day, even when it is so dark you can hardly see your canvas in the studio. You are going to be painting pictures to pay the bills". I nearly burst into tears; I thought I was going to be different because I was an Artist.

This discipline is something I have practised ever since and I am very grateful to Robin for teaching it to me. Being with Robin was fun, too. We went out into the streets of London, setting up our easels in Westminster Square and Piccadilly Circus. I had never painted in the fresh air before, not even in the middle of a field with no-one watching. It was a frightening experience to set up my easel on the pavement in London, with 200 people watching behind me.

My early career

After three years, Robin Goodwin said he couldn't teach me any more. My father let me live at home for the first twelve months and this meant that I did not actually have to earn my living straight away. It was a wonderful opportunity to paint pictures for myself. We were now living in Camberley, just a few miles away from Heathrow. I was still very interested in aeroplanes and the airport seemed a wonderful place to go and paint.

It was 1953 and Heathrow was not the concrete jungle it is now. Only a few aeroplanes landed every day and just a few people got off them. I was allowed to drive my car wherever I wanted. I set up my easel and canvas in the hangers, or in front of the many aeroplanes that were sitting around on the runways.

THE SURREY ADVERTISER AND COUNTY TIMES MARCH 20th 195

"Aircraft are beautiful" says this young artist

IF there had been a shortage of game wardens in Kenya, 22-year-old Mr David Shepherd, of Frimley Hall, Camberley, would never have become one of the foremost of the tiny group of artists specialising in painting aircraft.

Painting was just a hobby to Mr Shepherd (pictured here working at London Airport) when he went to Africa in 1950, but he returned to Britain nine months later determined to make it his career. After priviate tuition he began painting landscapes, nature studies, locomotives, cathedrals—and aircraft. "Get planes in the right postion and they are beautiful," he says. "Some of my fellow artists deliberately beautify them for commercial purposes; but I paint them as I see them on the ground and in the air."

It was a lovely hot summer. I painted about 30 pictures but I never sold any—I don't think the companies or the airlines were really very interested. I still have most of them in my collection.

I was still living at home in 1957 when I met a girl called Avril who was living in Camberley. We were married in that year. In 1958, the first of our four daughters was born. I was gradually beginning to be noticed as an artist. I even managed to sell enough paintings to pay the bills. My luck was beginning to turn.

1. Our wedding day

2. Our daughter, Mandy

3. Three of our daughters—
   Melinda, Mandy and Melanie.

4. Our daughter, Melanie

The turning point

It was in 1960 that a very important looking envelope dropped through my letterbox. It was from the Commander-in-Chief of the Royal Air Force in British Forces Arabian Peninsula, from their headquarters in Aden. He had read an article in a magazine about my aeroplane paintings and wanted to invite me out to Aden as his personal guest.

He did not promise me any work when I arrived in Aden. It was up to me to meet all the squadron commanders and wait to see what would happen. However, this did seem a wonderful chance to help my career forward and I set off full of excitement.

I flew to Aden in a Royal Air Force Comet. When I arrived, I was treated like a VIP (Very Important Person). I was driven around in a car which belonged to the Commander-in-Chief himself. However, from the very moment I arrived, it seemed that the Royal Air Force Squadrons in Aden were not at all interested in artists. A big dinner party was thrown in my honour but still no one wanted my work. It was decided that I would fly back to England again on the first available Royal Air Force aeroplane.

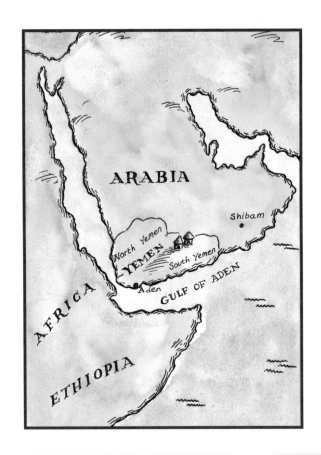

No flight was going back to England for a week, so I decided to explore. I found an amazing place called Slave Island. Here, the Arab boat builders built old-fashioned fishing vessels that sailed the spice routes of the Arabian seas, just as they did in the days of the Bible. It seemed that nothing had changed since then. I set up my easel in front of this wonderful subject and I painted the whole picture in oils. The painting took five days to do. When I showed it to the Commander-in-Chief he was so pleased he decided to have a party to celebrate! At that party I received 48 orders for further paintings.

'Slave Island'

'Shibam'

Even more important, they decided to fly me all over the interior of Arabia. I saw places that excited me beyond belief, like the skyscraper city called Shibam, all made in mud bricks, which had not changed over the centuries. No Europeans lived there. There was no electricity and there were no motor cars.

However, that was not all. The Royal Air Force also flew me to Kenya. They asked me whether I had ever painted animals. I hadn't even painted a hamster before, but I didn't mind having a go. So I went to Nairobi to buy a canvas and I painted my very first wildlife painting, for the Royal Air Force. It was a great success and suddenly everybody wanted my animal paintings. It has been like that ever since.

My first wildlife painting

Becoming a conservationist

Something else happened during the visit to Nairobi in 1960. Avril and I flew down to Tanzania, to the Serengeti National Park for a few days' holiday. We went out very early one morning in the game warden's Landrover® and we saw, over the horizon, hundreds of vultures circling in the sky.

Vultures are the most wonderful birds; they are known as 'nature's dustmen'. They keep Africa clean and they are all part of the wonderful balance of nature. When lions have been on a kill and they move away, the vultures come down from circling above and eat up all the remains, leaving the ground clean and tidy. However, I remember the warden saying on this occasion, "David, this is something different. There is something wrong and we had better go over and see what has happened".

We found a water hole that had been poisoned by a poacher and 255 dead zebra were lying on the ground. That was the moment that I became a conservationist.

In 1971, I met Neil Armstrong. It was very exciting to meet him because in 1969 Neil Armstrong was the first man to walk on the Moon. I was introduced to him at a party as a conservationist.

He said, "David, I am a conservationist too, you have to be when you have been to the Moon and back. As I was coming back from the Moon in my space capsule, I looked through the window at planet Earth. I saw it floating all by itself in space, looking very lonely and very small." He then went on, "When I saw planet Earth floating in space all by itself, about the size of a golf ball, it looked very fragile." When a man has travelled 250,000 miles away from planet Earth on the end of a rocket, and walked on the Moon and come home again, it must mean something when he talks like that. It is the only world we have, and it is fragile.

My life now

My paintings of animals have earned me a lot of money. In 1962 Avril and I were able to buy a lovely, four-hundred-year-old farmhouse. We are still living there. Badgers, deer and foxes come to our large garden and we have a beautiful lake which all the birds love.

I also own and run two enormous steam engines. I bought them from British Railways and restored them. Now they run on a railway in Somerset which I set up. This gives a lot of pleasure to many visitors.

1. Our farmhou

2. Me with my four daughte

3. One of my steam engin

26

I have been a lucky man, and I owe it all to the animals I paint. When I saw the dead zebra in 1960 I realized for the first time that man is the most dangerous animal on earth. Many years ago, when I was a child, people did not know or care about what was going on. Now, young children know that rainforests are being destroyed and that animals are being killed for their fur or their bones. I have seen some terrible things, and I wanted to do something about it.

So in 1985, The David Shepherd Conservation Foundation was set up. This is a small charity based in the farmhouse which my daughter, Melanie, runs with three other people. Over the last few years we have donated over £1.4 million to help save the tiger, the rhino, the elephant and many other endangered mammals.

The remains of an elephant left by a poacher.

My life now is very exciting and rewarding. I often travel to Africa and India to raise more money for wildlife. At other times, I go to the national parks to see my friends, the elephants.

I sometimes stay in Botswana, at a camp far away from anywhere. When it has not rained there for many months, the area is like a desert. The only water hole is an artificial one near the camp, where the water is pumped up through the ground. The elephants found this many years ago and they come every year in the dry season.

When Avril and I were there last time, it seemed as if they were waiting for me! I was able to sit just three metres away from 25 huge bull elephants drinking the water. They were very thirsty and took no notice of me at all. They had no reason to be frightened because they were protected. They had never been shot at by their most dangerous enemy, man. It is a wonderful feeling to be able to sit so close to a wild animal.

Only one world

We have only one world and we share it with all other living creatures, the trees, the birds, the animals and the insects. They depend on us and we depend on them. Neither can do without the other.

When I first went to Zambia in Africa, there were 3500 rhinos there. Now there are none left. I want my grandchildren to be able to see tigers in India, or elephants in Africa and I wonder if it will still be possible.

Conservation isn't just about saving rhinos and tigers. It is about saving and looking after trees, green fields and hedgerows, as well as the hot dusty plains of Africa and the frozen wastes of the Arctic. It is the young people of this world who can really begin to do something about it.

'The Ivory is theirs'

I will finish by telling a true story about a twelve year old girl who decided to help elephants although she had never been to Africa. She knew that elephants were in trouble, because there are men who steal ivory to make money. She decided to get on her bicycle and ride across England from west to east, across the widest part, being sponsored all the way. She sent the Conservation foundation over £1000.00 to help save the elephant.

I will always remember that girl, and will give her a big hug if I meet her. That is what conservation is all about.

Index

Aden 18–19

aeroplanes 4, 16–18

Africa 3, 5, 6–12, 22, 28–31

Amboseli 9

Arabia 20–21

art school 12

artist 2, 5, 12–14, 19

Avril 17, 22, 26, 29

Botswana 28

coffee farm 7

conservation 23–25, 31

David Shepherd
Conservation Foundation 27, 31

elephants 2, 8–9, 27–31

game warden 2, 3, 5, 8–9, 12, 22

Heathrow 16

Hendon 4

Indian Ocean 11

Kenya 2, 6–11, 21

Malindi 9

mallards 11

Mount Kilimanjaro 9

Nairobi 7–9, 21–22

Neil Armstrong 24–25

Robin Goodwin 13–16

Slave Island 20

Tanzania 22

Totteridge 4

vultures 22

wildlife 21, 28–29

World War II 4

zebra 23, 27

'Rhino Reverie'